1001 ILLUMINATED INITIAL LETTERS

INITIAL LETTERS

27 FULL-COLOR PLATES

BY OWEN JONES

DOVER PUBLICATIONS, INC., NEW YORK

Published in Canada by General Publishing Company, Ltd., 30 Lesmill Road, Don Mills, Toronto, Ontario.
Published in the United Kingdom by Constable and Company, Ltd.

This Dover edition, first published in 1988, is an unabridged reproduction of all the plates of *One Thousand and One Initial Letters Designed and Illuminated by Owen Jones* (originally published by Day & Son, London) as published in Germany by Ludwig Denicke, Leipzig, 1864. The letterpress title page to the German edition is here omitted.

DOVER *Pictorial Archive* SERIES

Manufactured in the United States of America
Dover Publications, Inc., 31 East 2nd Street, Mineola, N.Y. 11501

Library of Congress Cataloging-in-Publication Data

Jones, Owen, 1809–1874.
    [One thousand and one initial letters]
    1001 illuminated initial letters : 27 full-color plates / by Owen Jones
        p.   cm. —(Dover pictorial archive series)
    Reprint. Originally published: One thousand and one initial letters. London : Day & Son, 1864.
    ISBN 0-486-25607-3 (pbk.)
    1. Initials. 2. Alphabets. 3. Decoration and ornament, Victorian. 4. Illumination of books and manuscripts. I. Title. II. Title: One thousand and one illuminated initial letters. III. Series.
NK3625.V53J66   1988
745.6'197'0924—dc19   87-36492
                                                             CIP

PUBLISHER'S NOTE

N RESPONSE to the harsh regimentation imposed by the Industrial Revolution on many aspects of life, artists and craftsmen of the nineteenth century looked to the examples of the past as they tried to reassert the individuality of the artist. The Middle Ages, especially the Gothic Period, was a source of major inspiration to them, for its spirituality exercised potent attractions.

Starting in the mid-eighteenth century, the Gothic Revival made its influence felt throughout the arts, from architecture and carpentry to book production. Of those who worked in calligraphy and typography, William Morris is perhaps most famous, but many others made distinctive contributions. Owen Jones (1809–1874), noted for his *The Grammar of Ornament* (the plates of which have been reproduced by Dover Publications, 25463-1), executed illuminations, predating Morris' work, that were particularly influential. Many of the letters appearing in *One Thousand and One Initial Letters* had been previously published in *The Psalms of David Illustrated by Owen Jones* (the "Victoria Psalter"), 1861. Far from slavish copies of the Gothic, they demonstrate a fecundity of imagination that makes them as vivid today as when they were first designed.

ONE
THOUSAND
AND ONE

Initial Letters

Designed and Illuminated

by

OWEN JONES

DAY & SON
LITHOGRAPHERS TO THE QUEEN
LONDON, 1864.

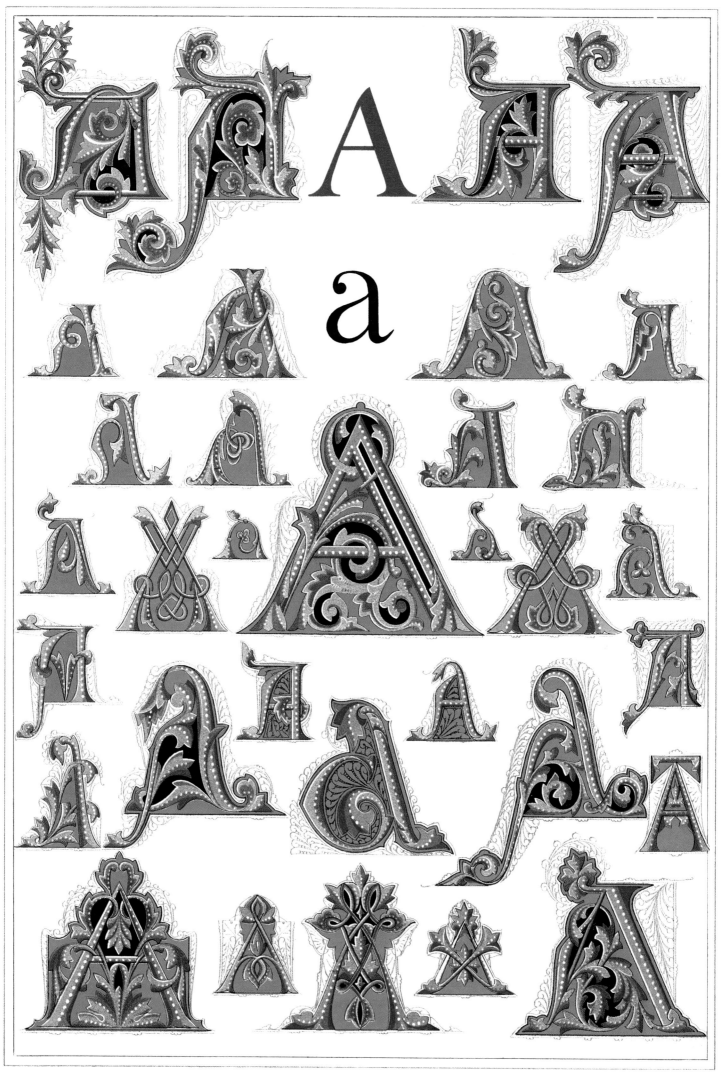

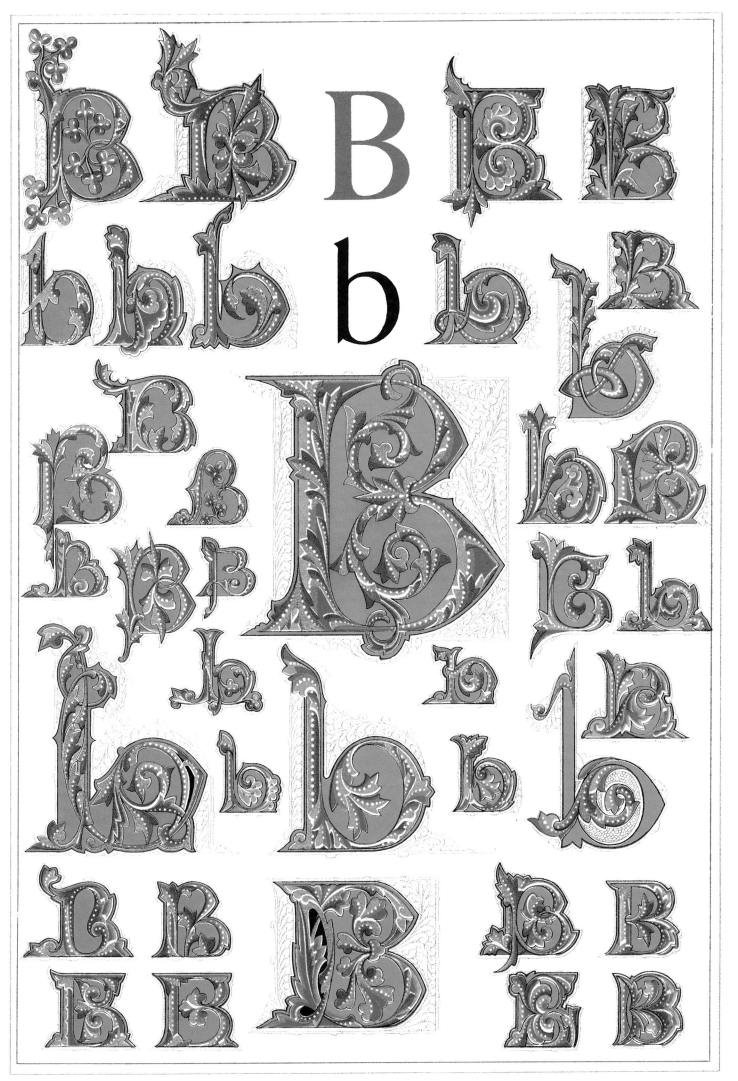

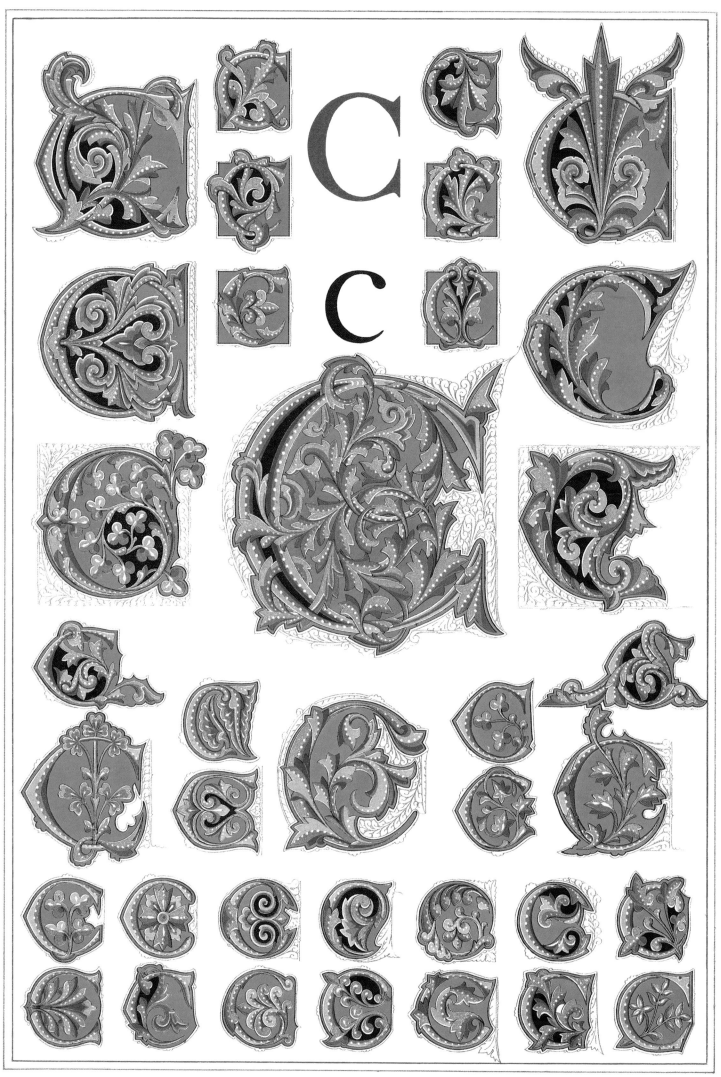

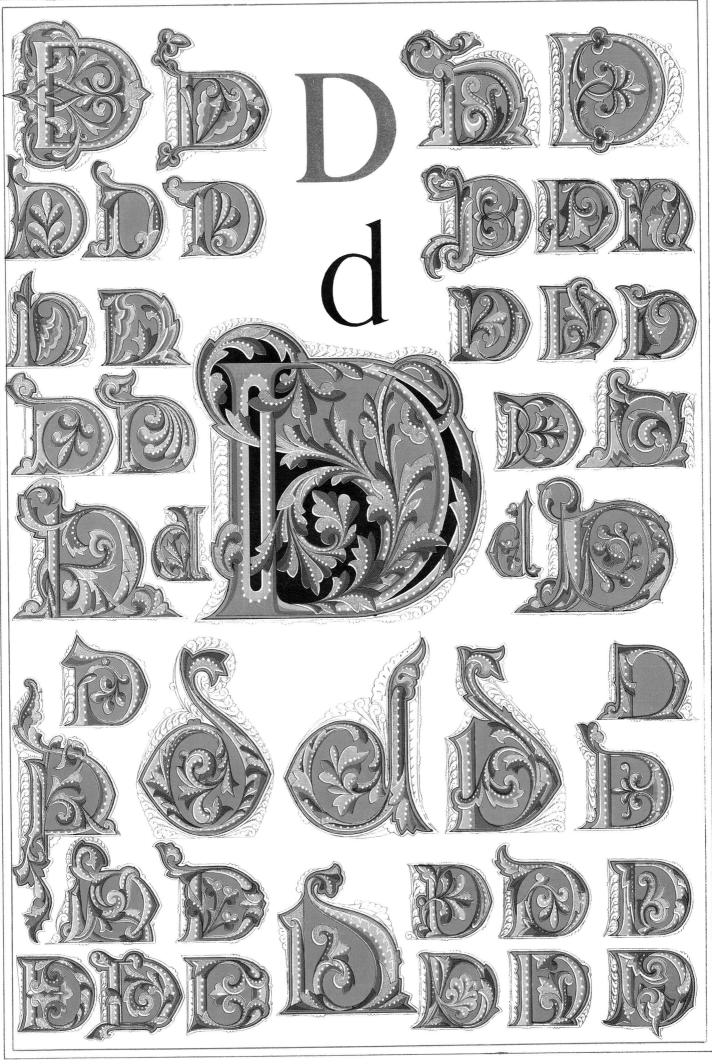

E e

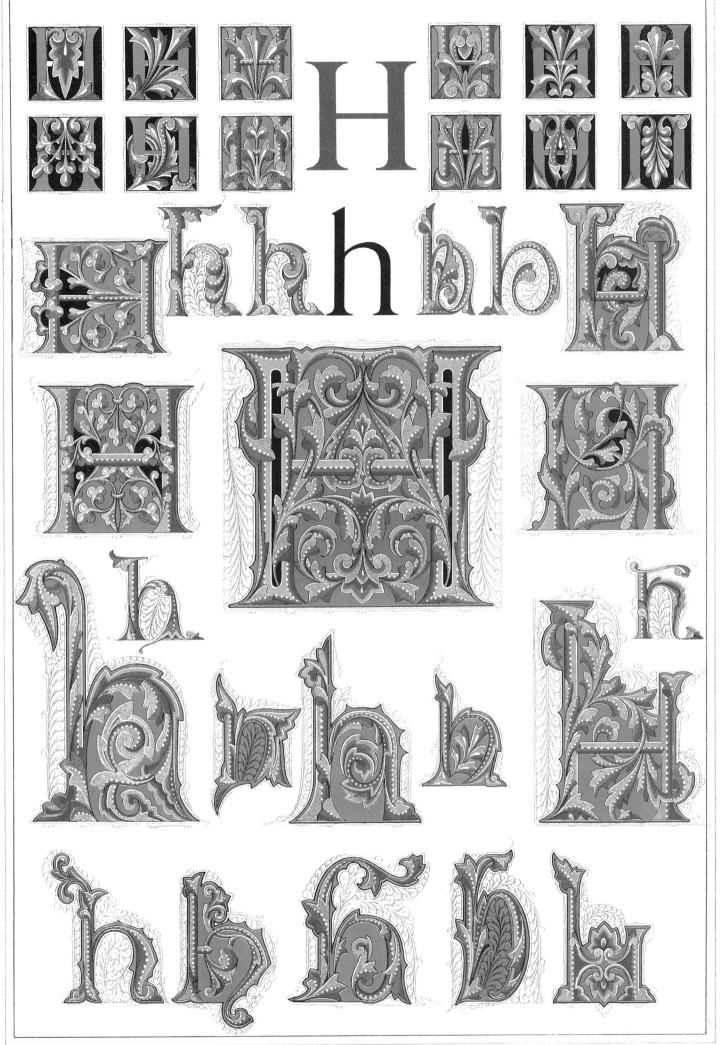

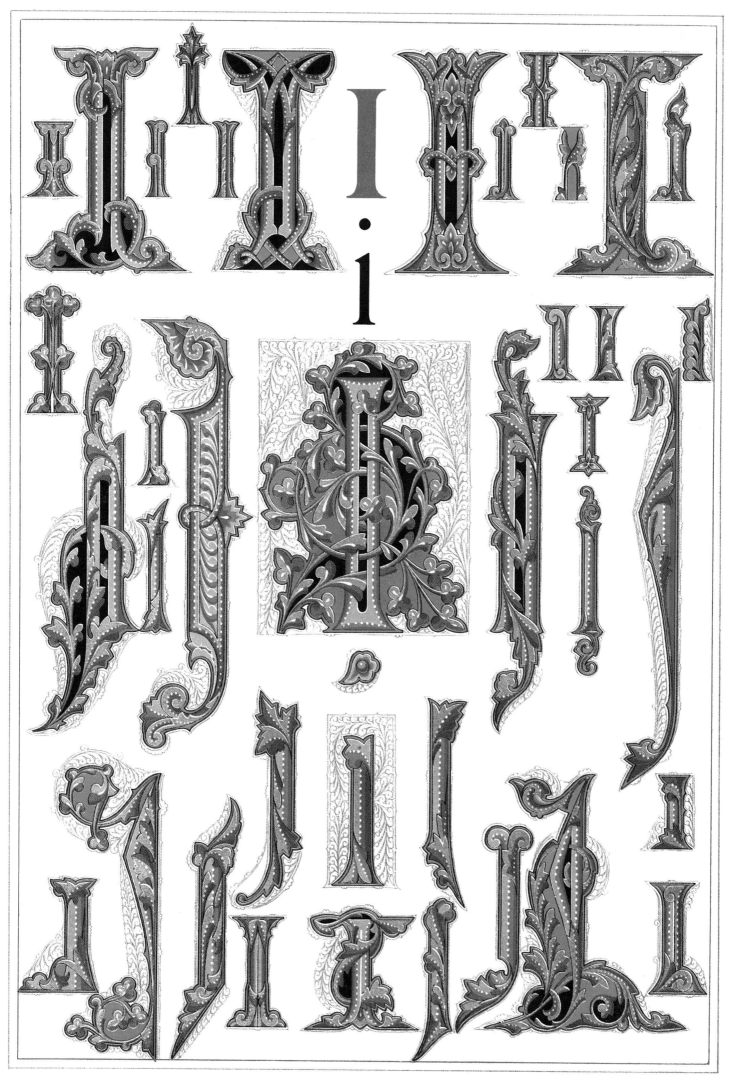

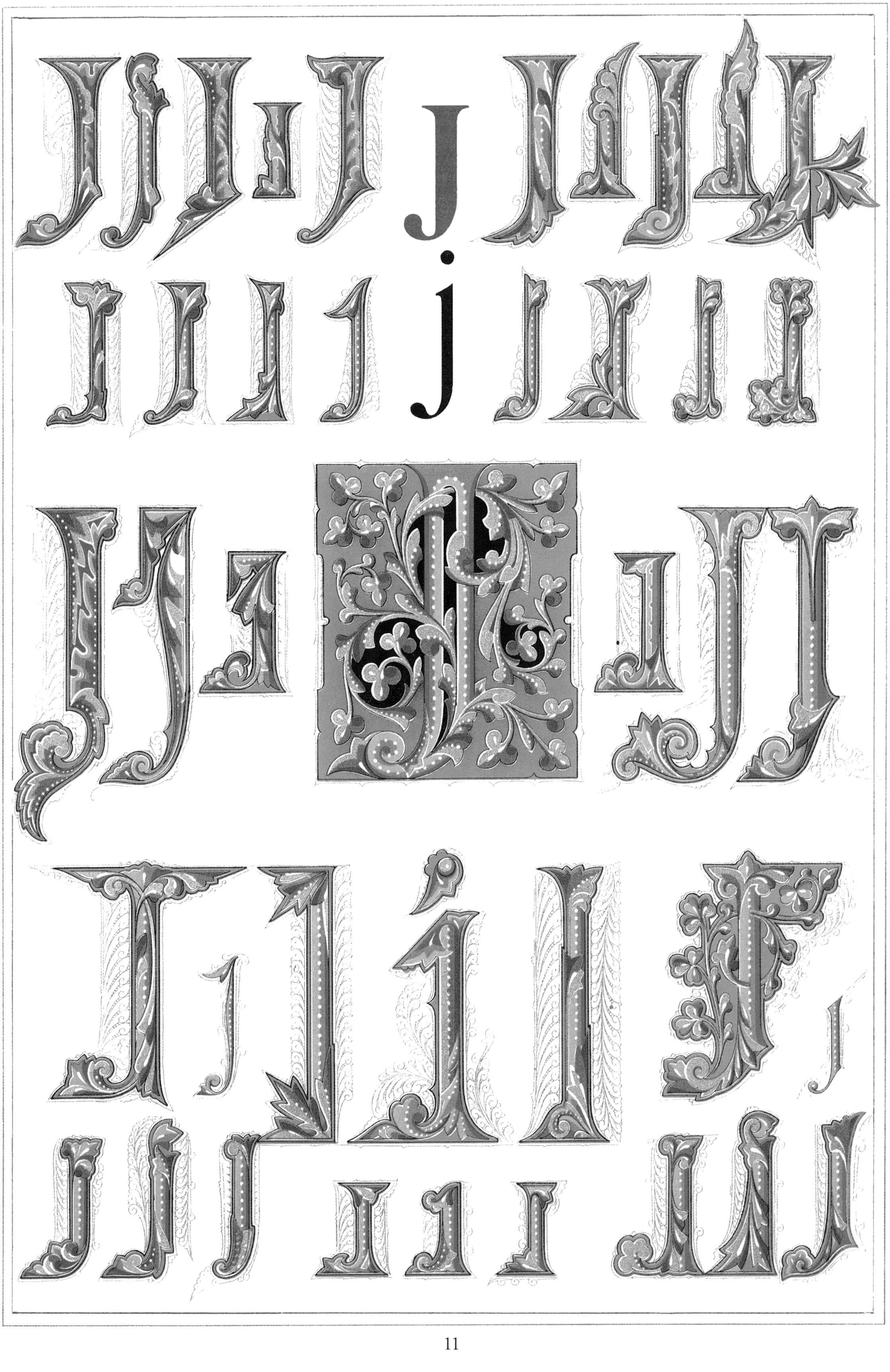

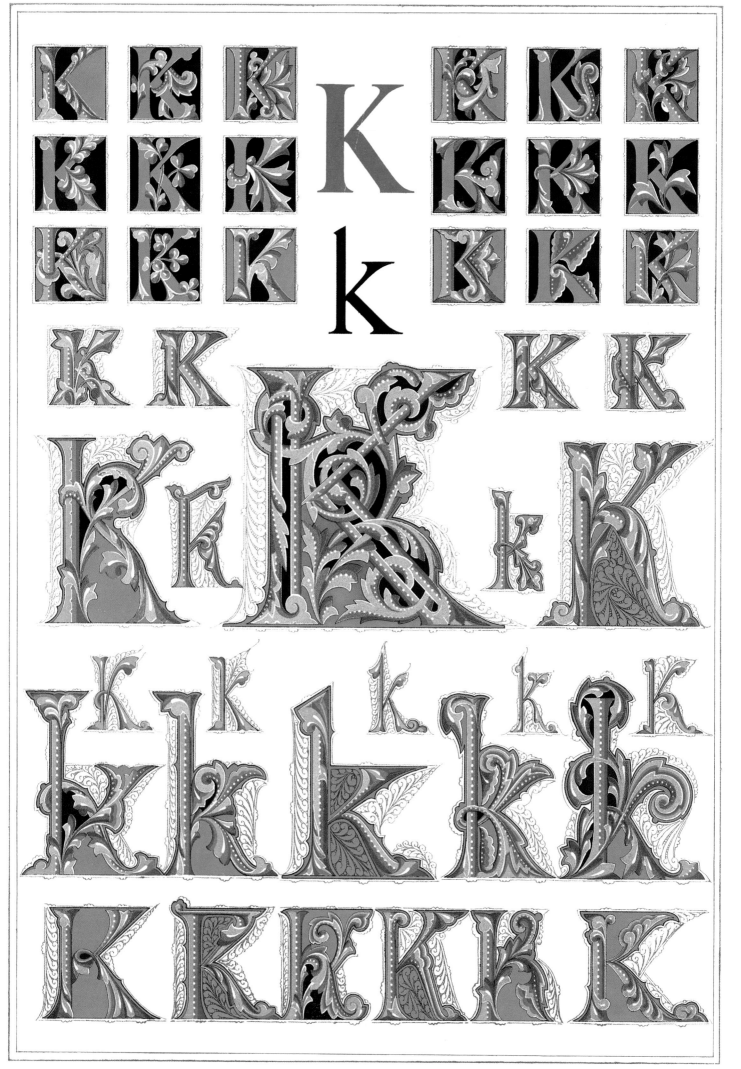

12

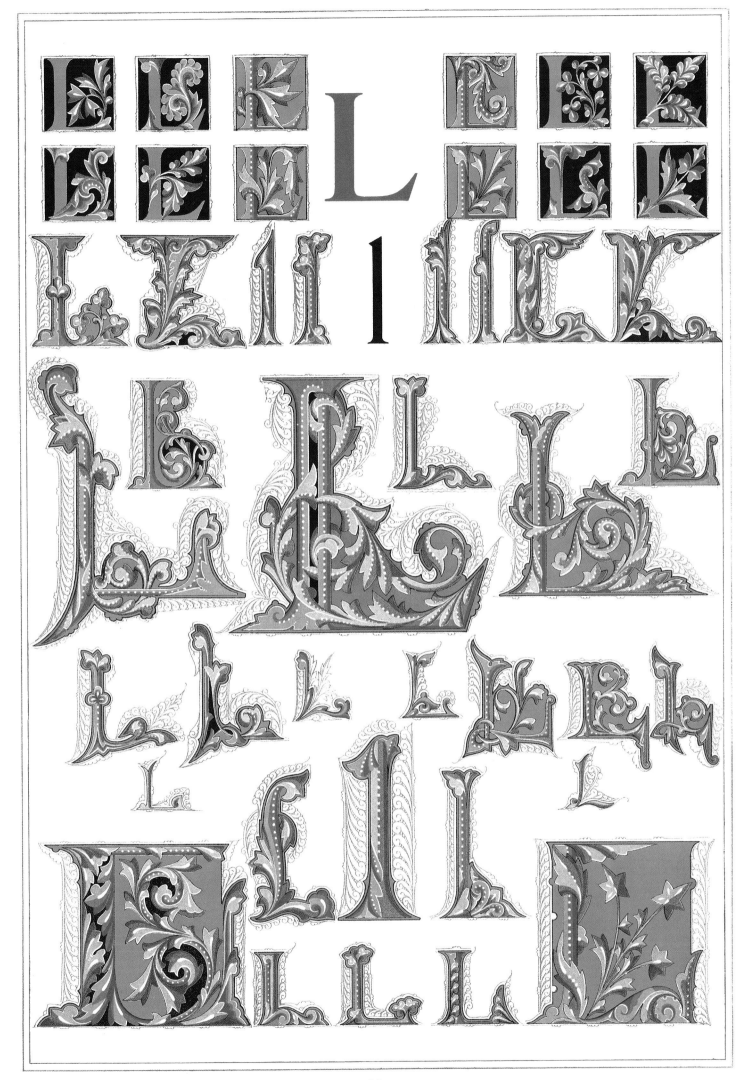

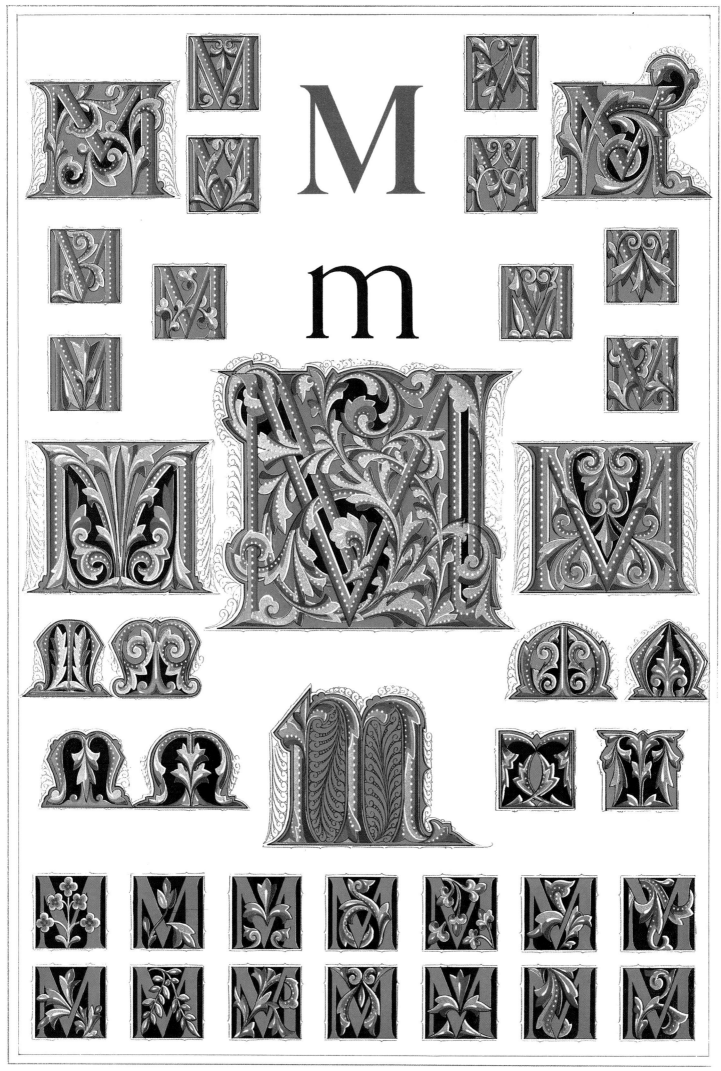

14

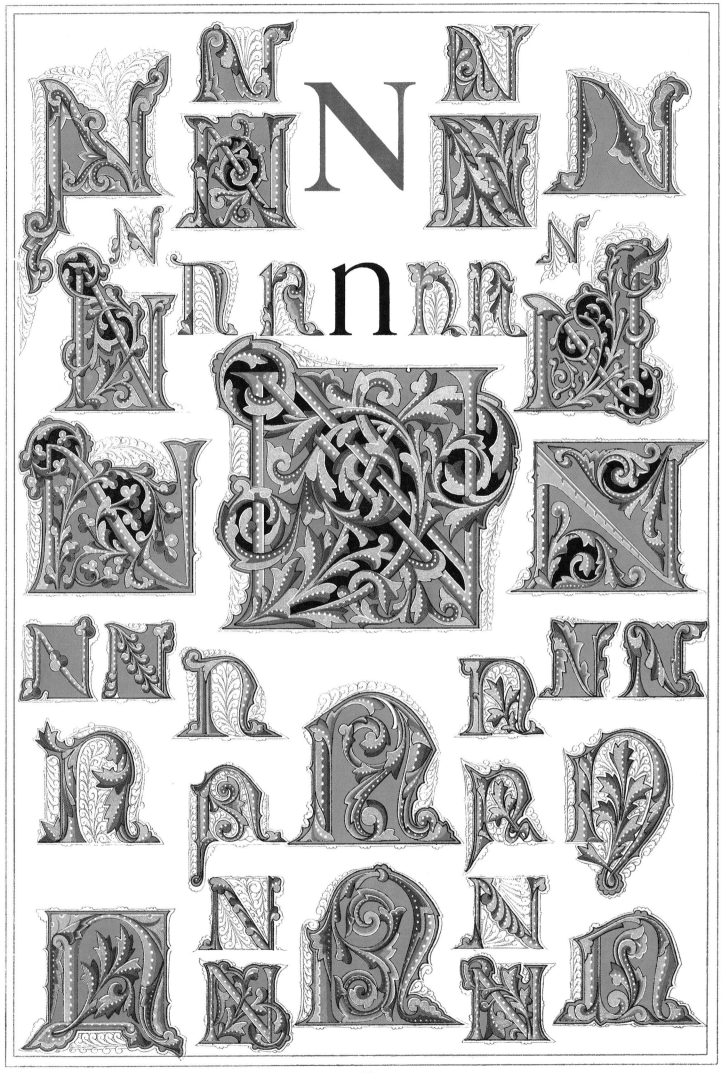

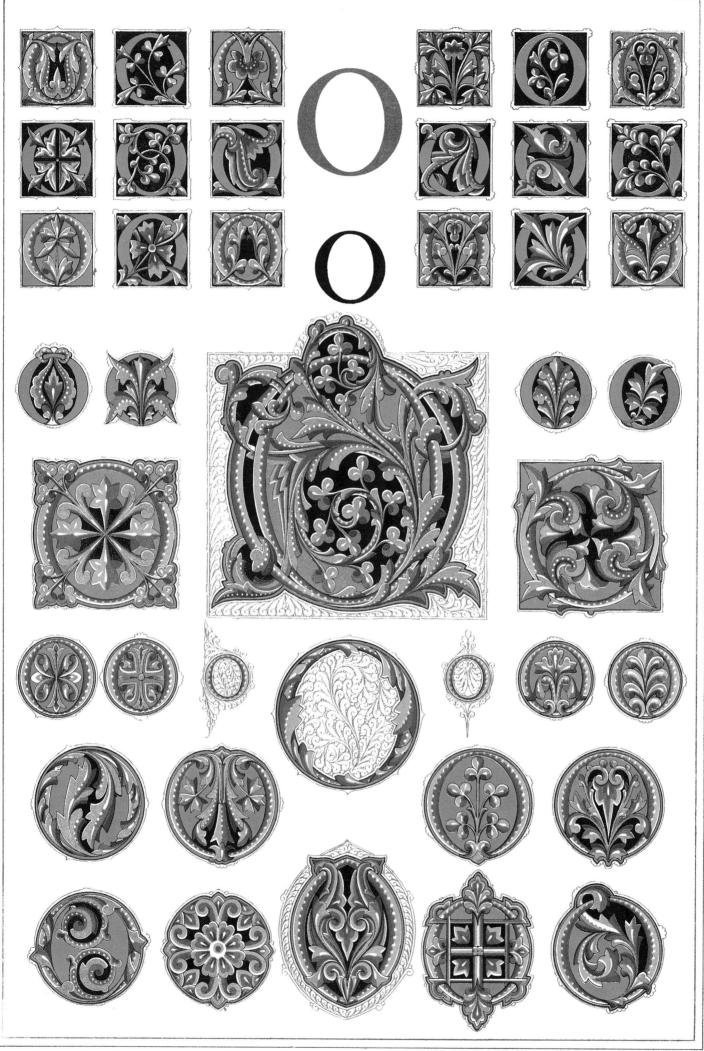

16

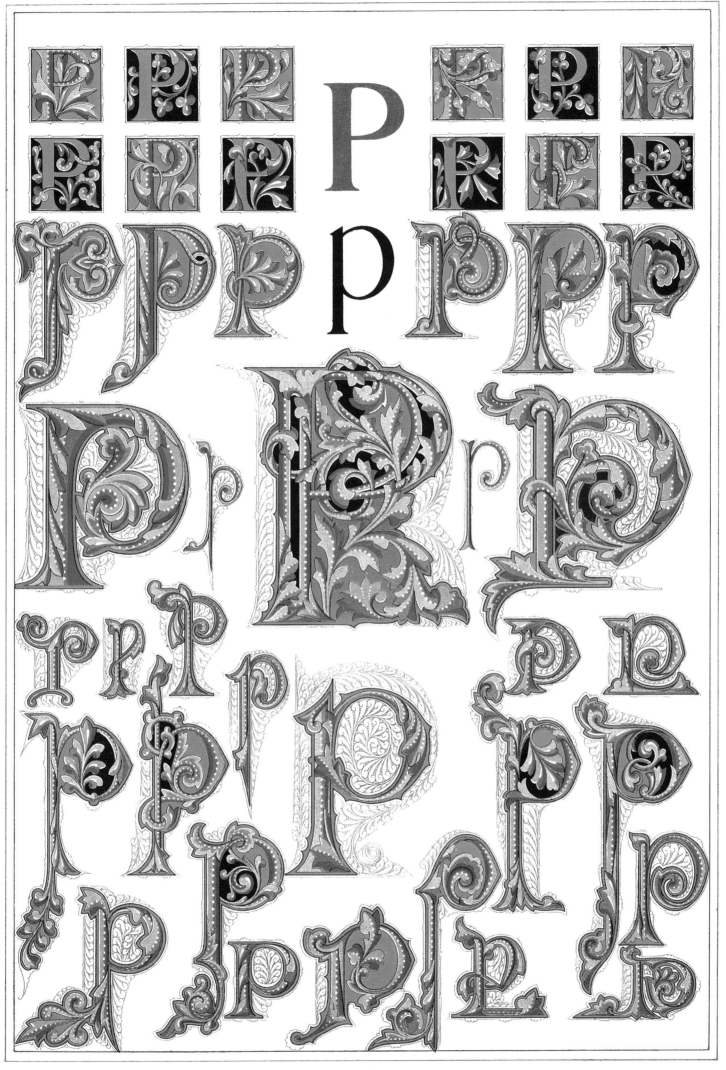

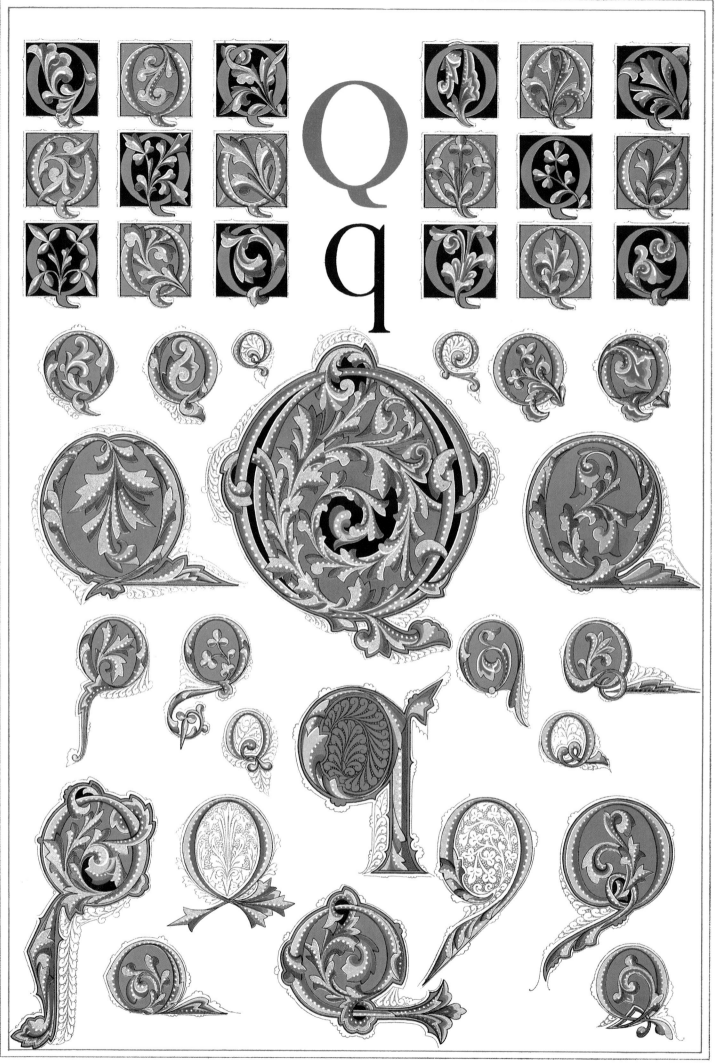

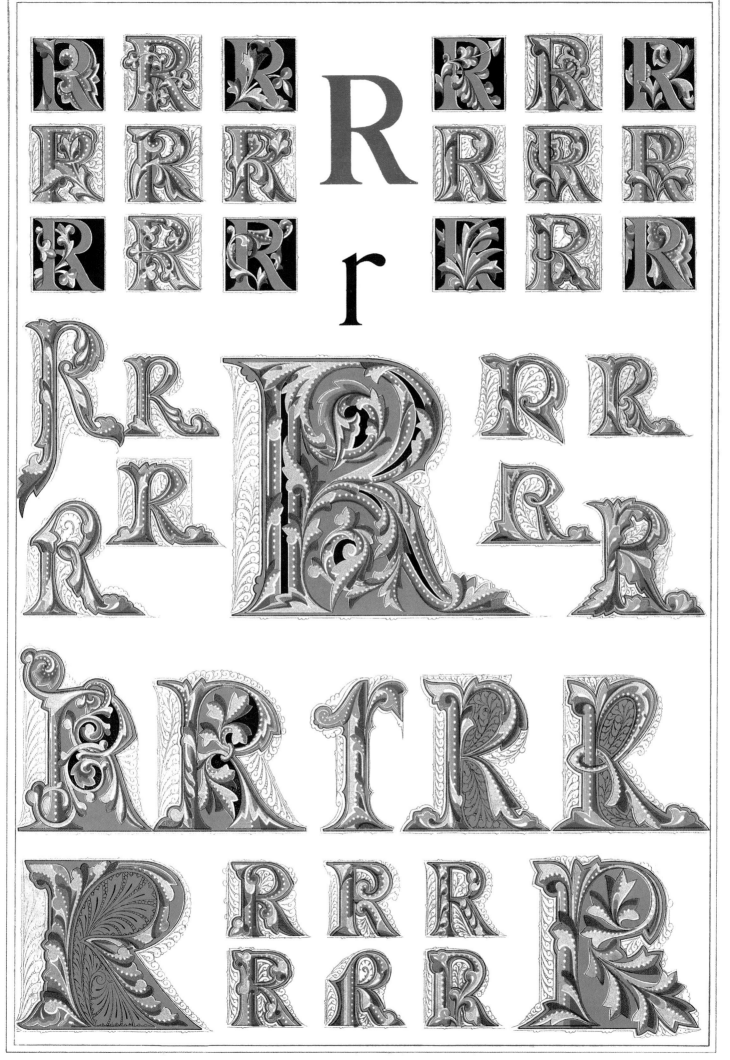

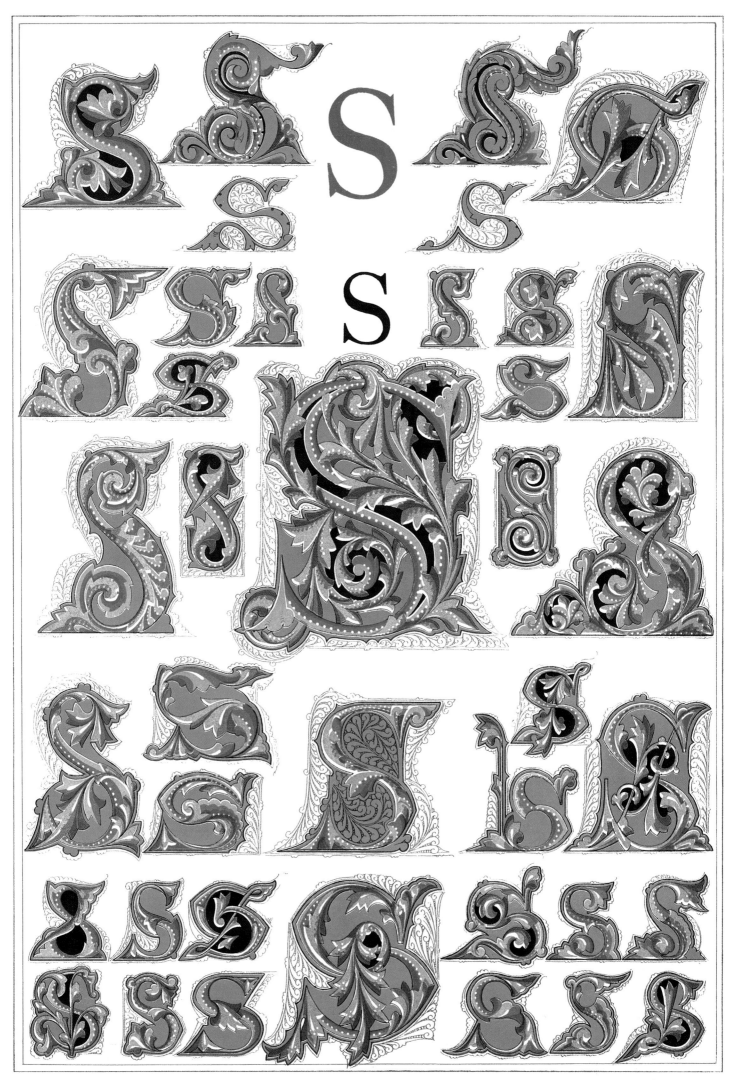

20

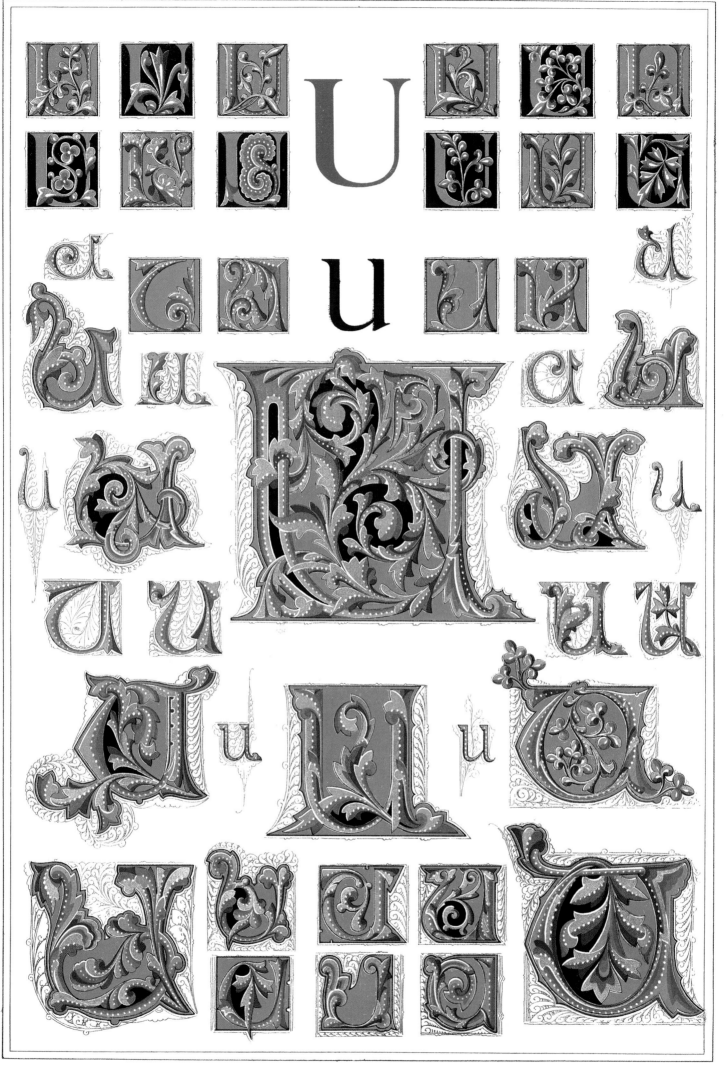

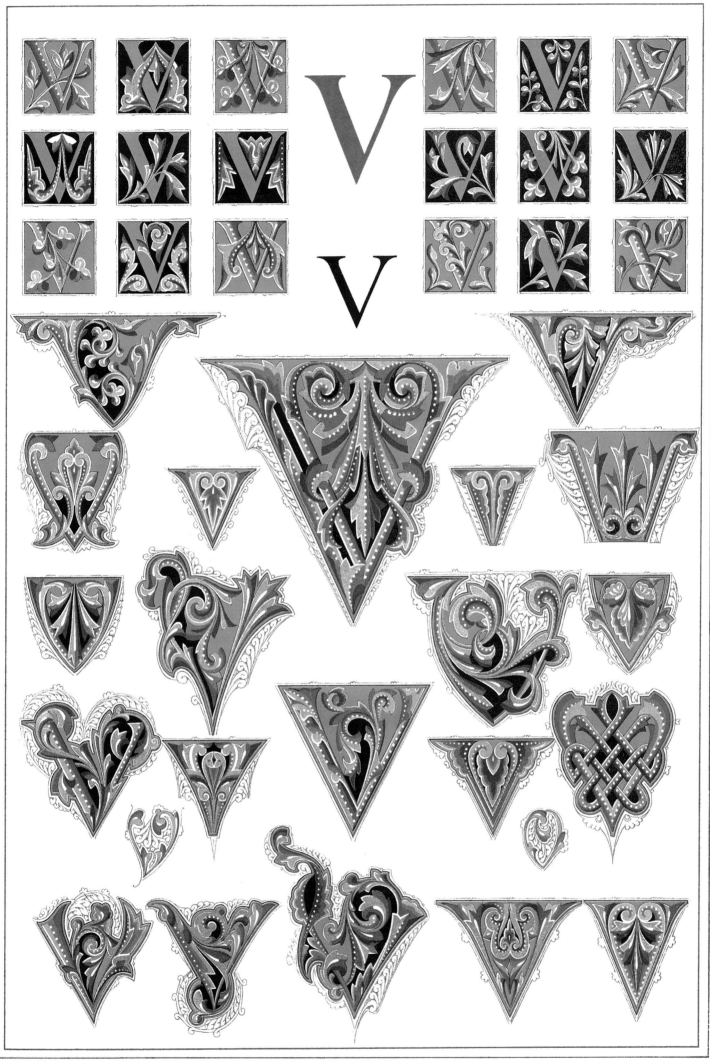

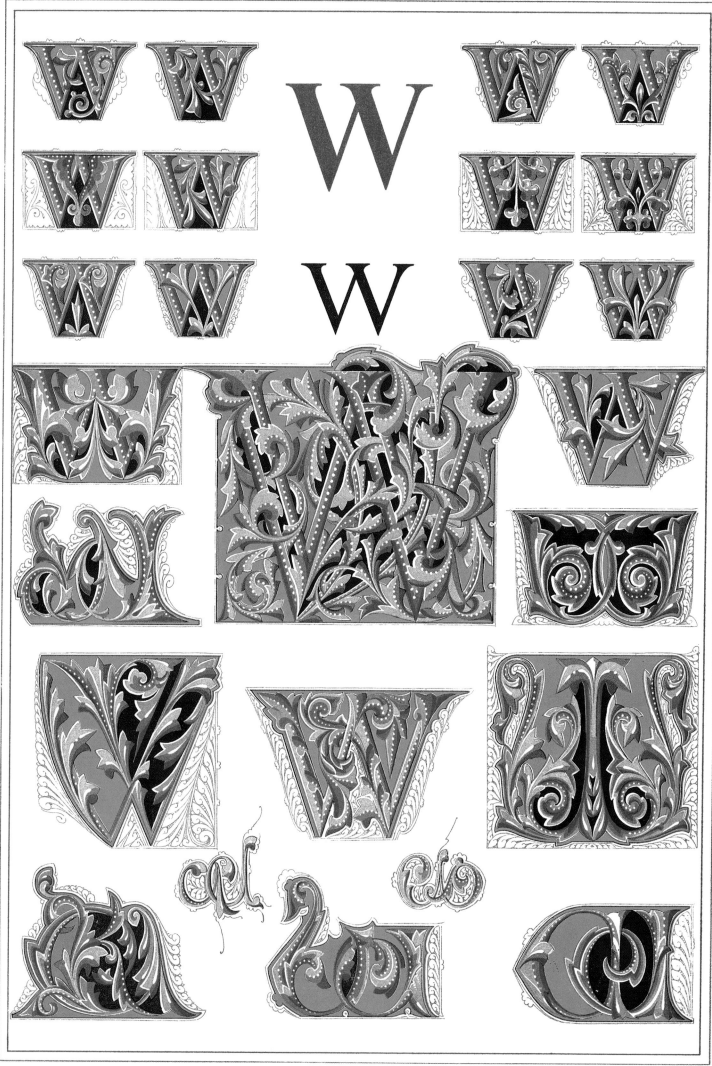

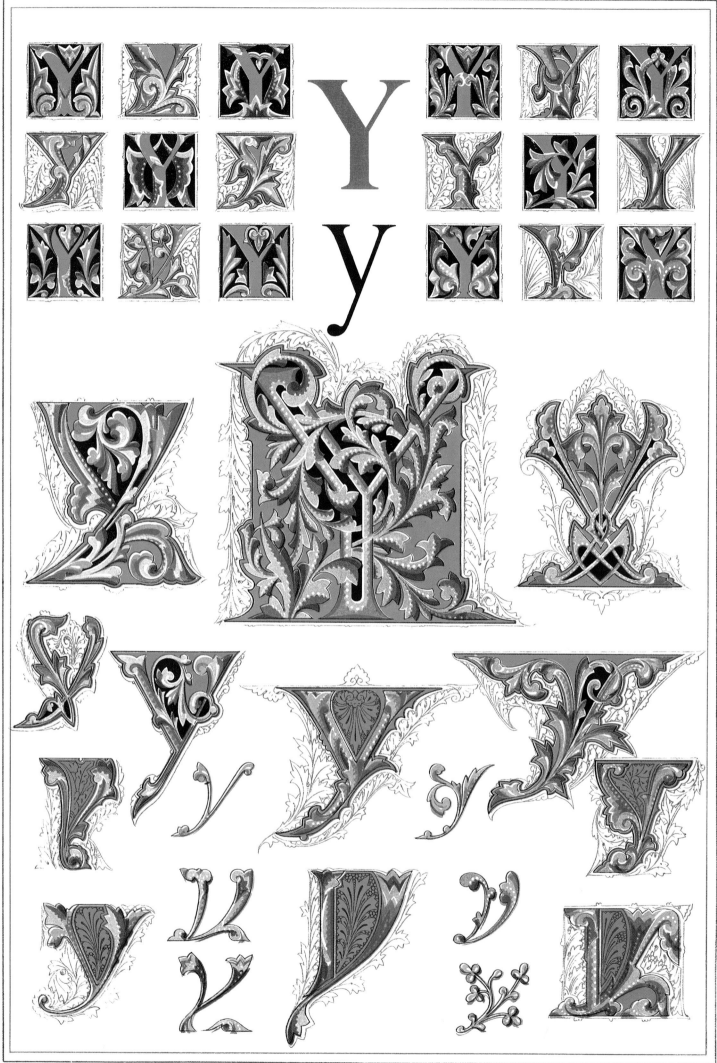

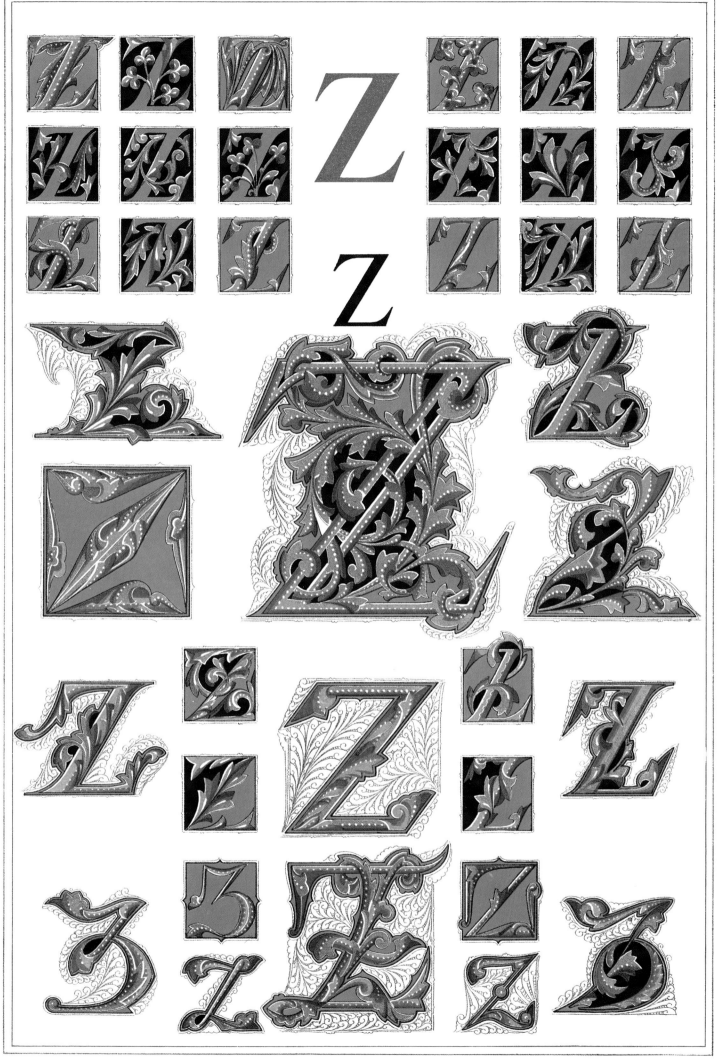

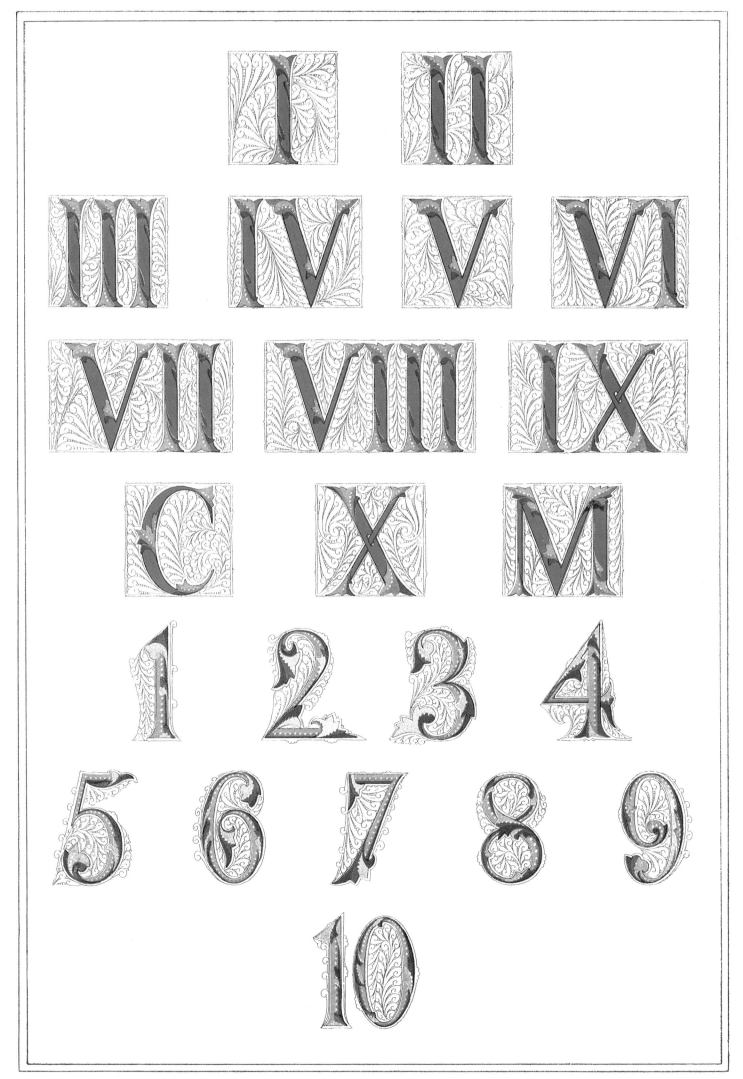